Welcome to Cozy Country Home Coloring Book

By: AH64Designs

Inside you will find
20 full pages of cozy country home coloring art.

Never stop having fun

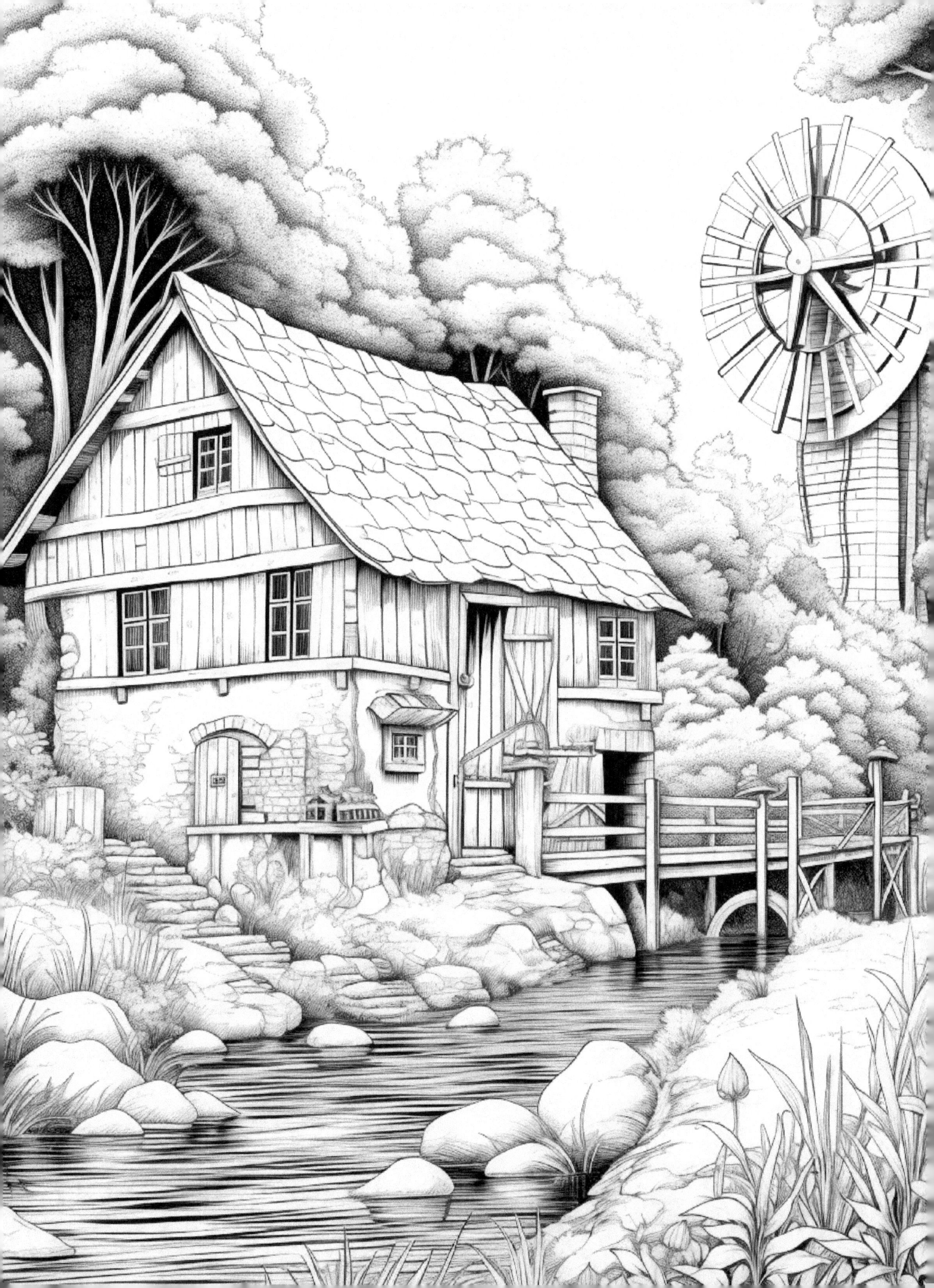

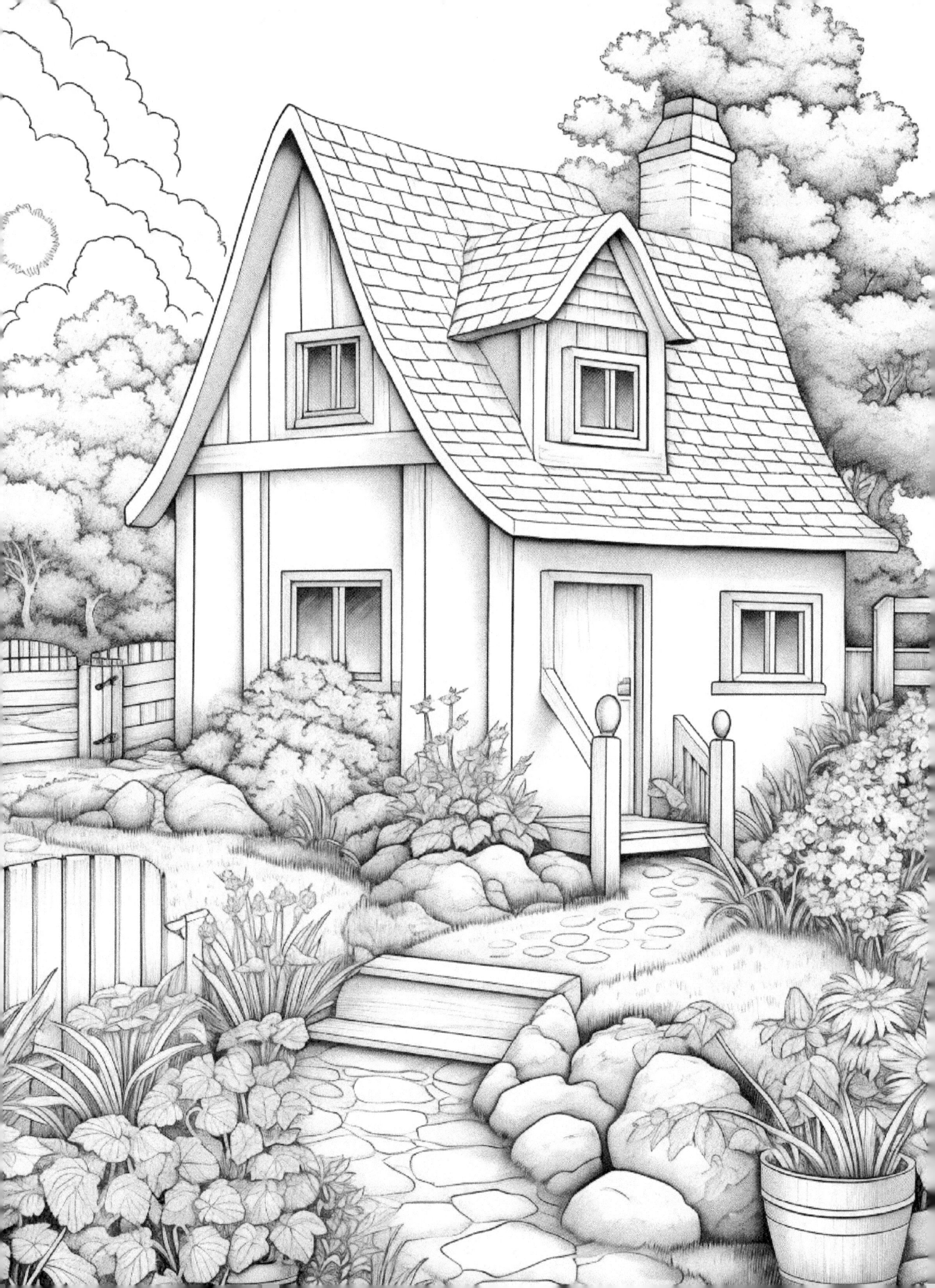

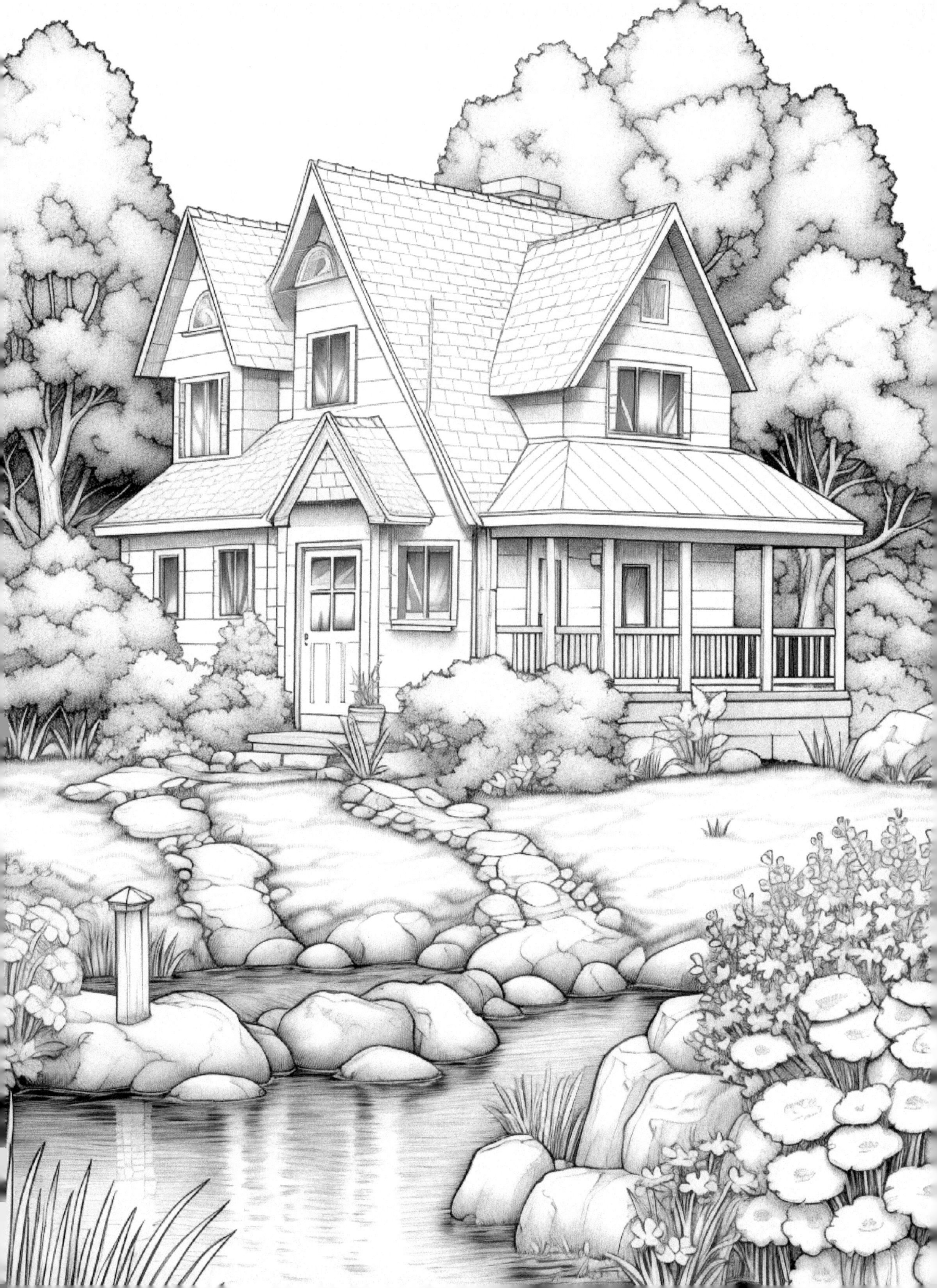

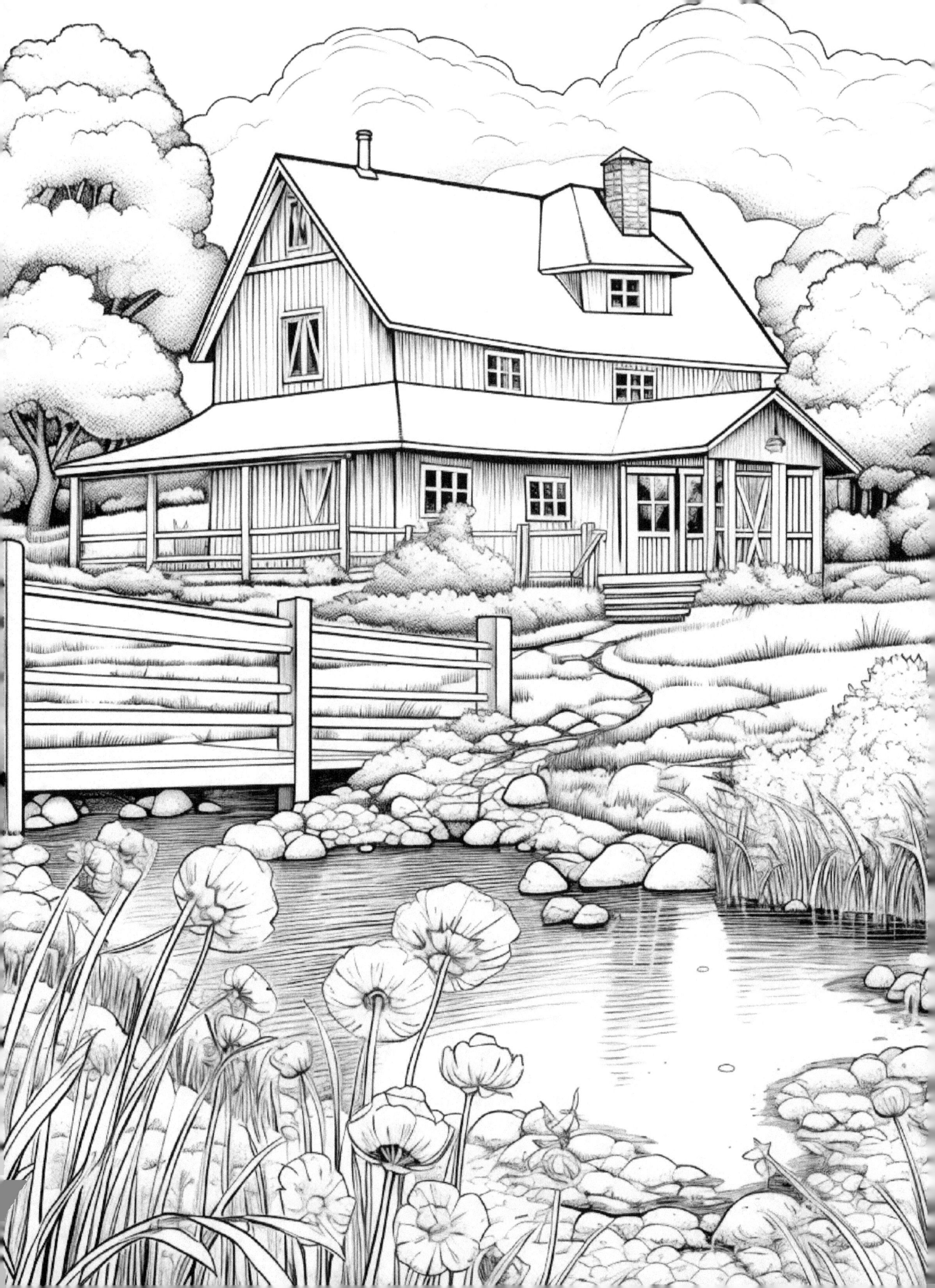

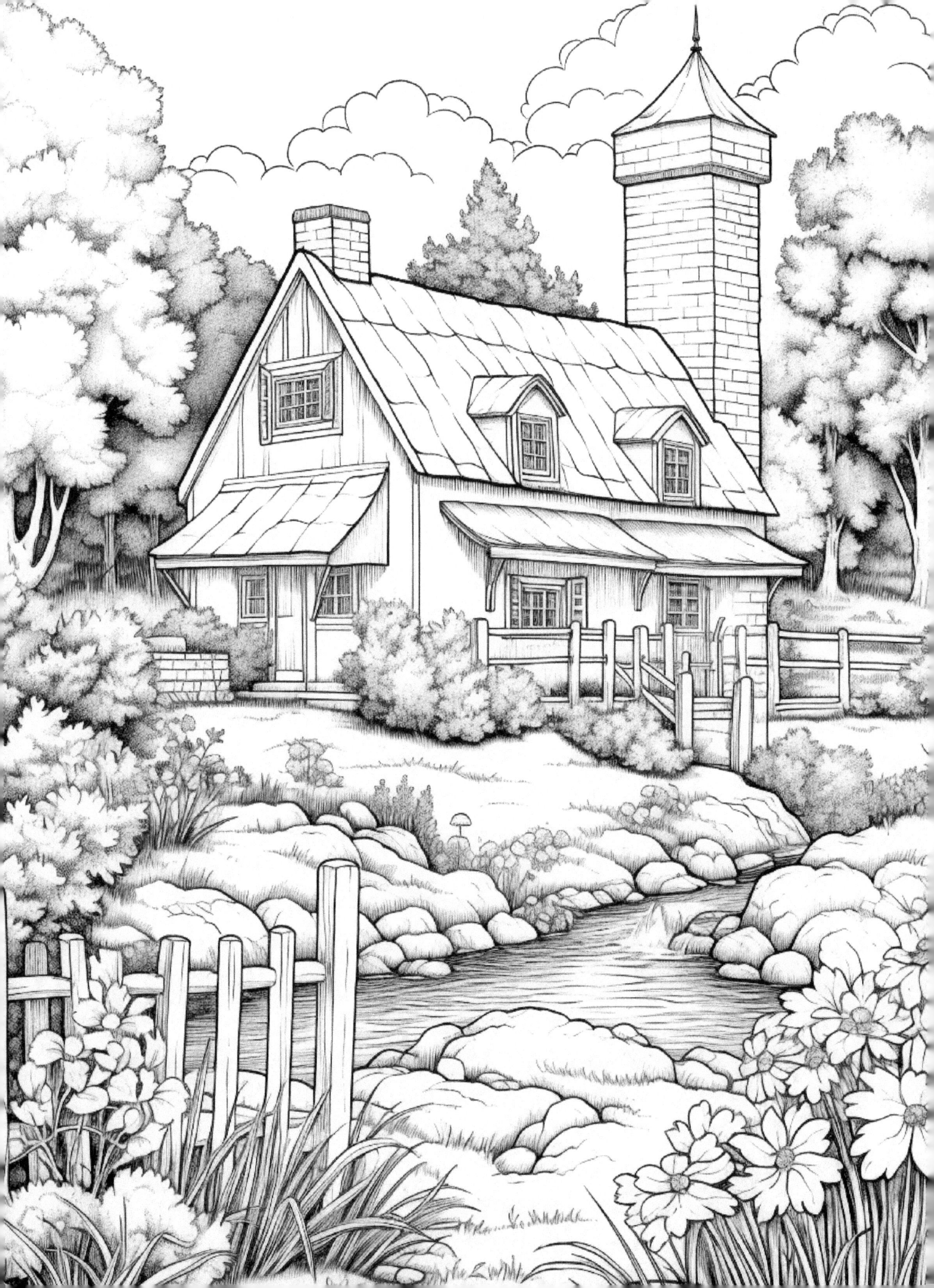

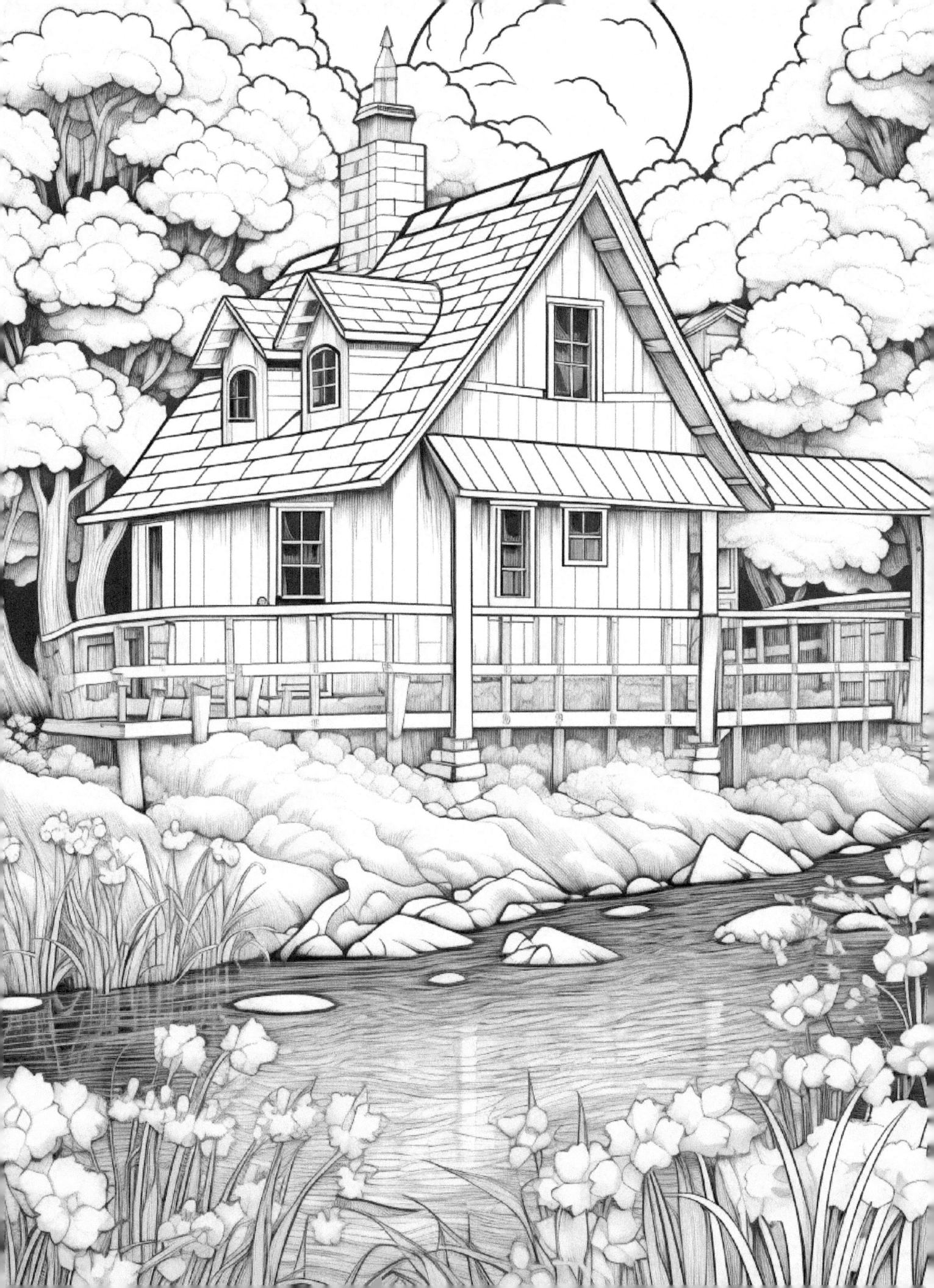

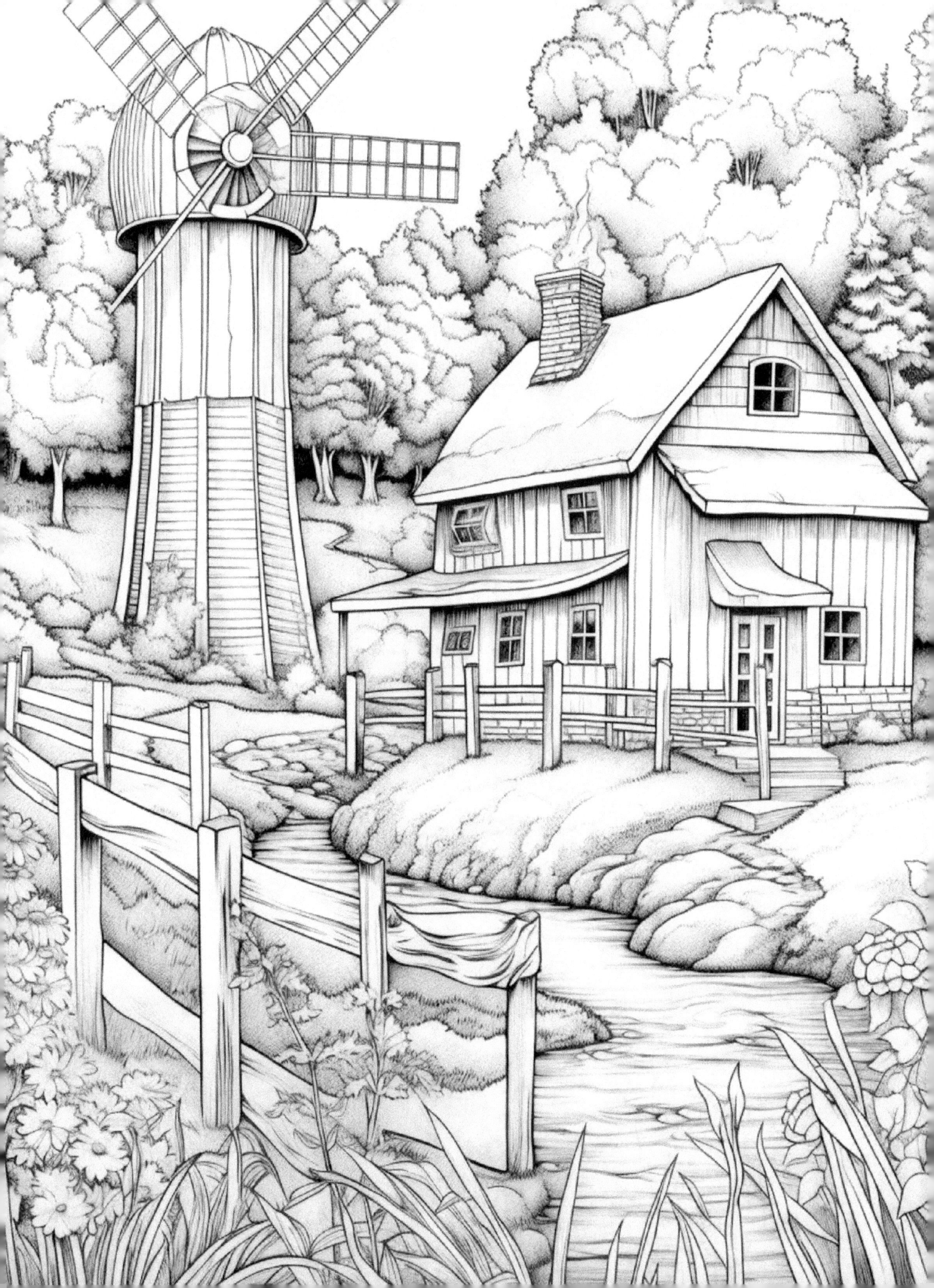

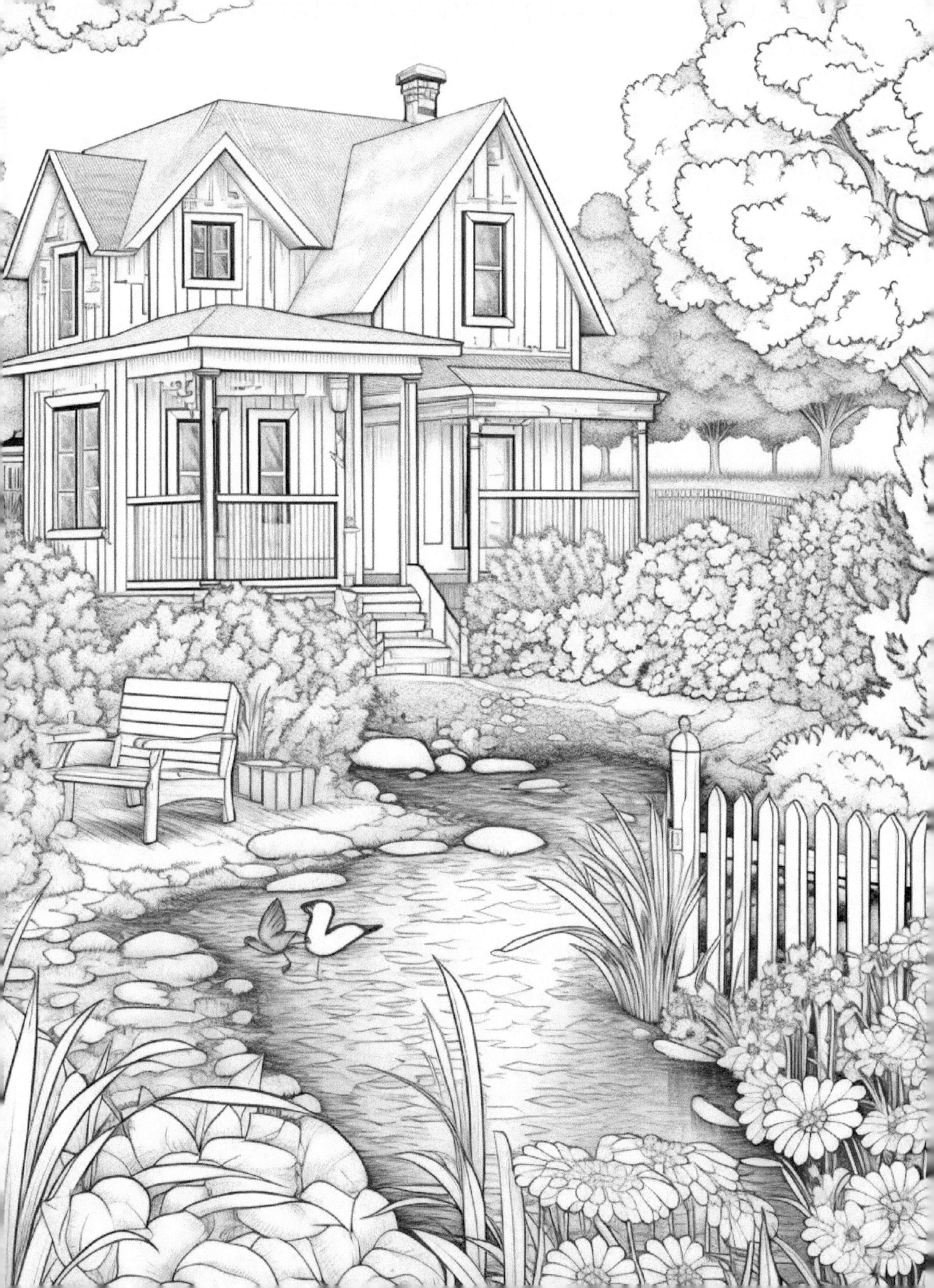

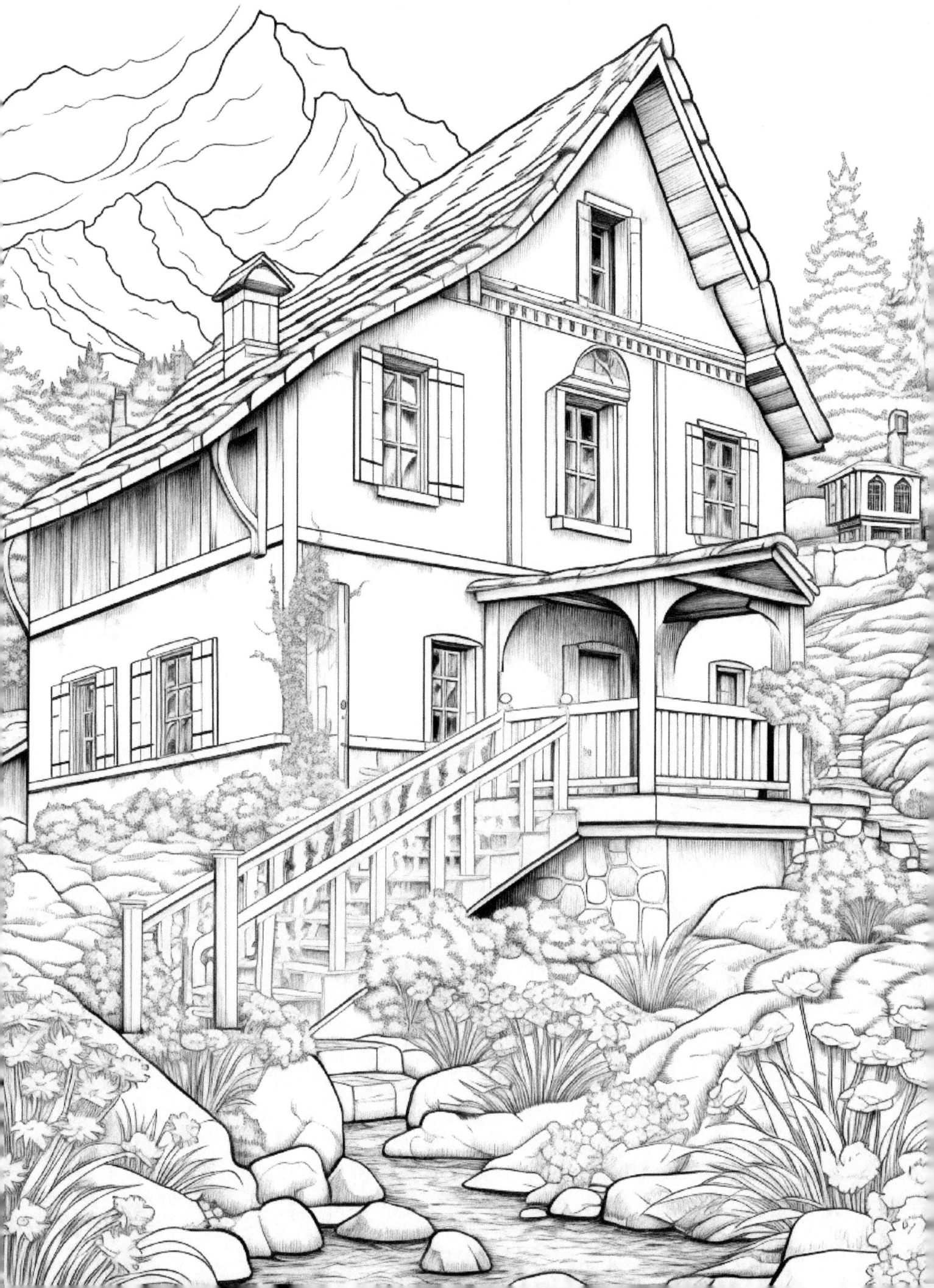

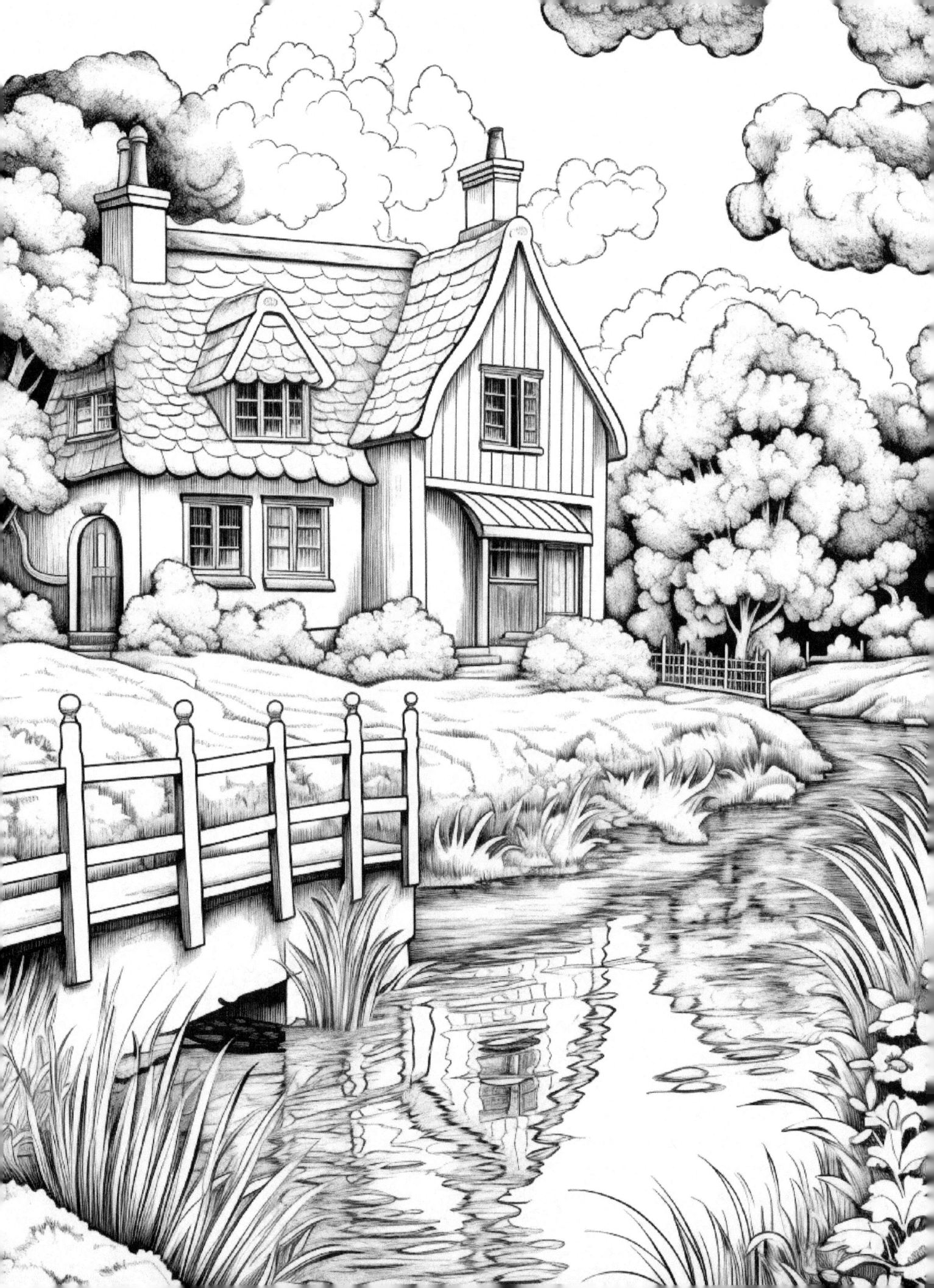

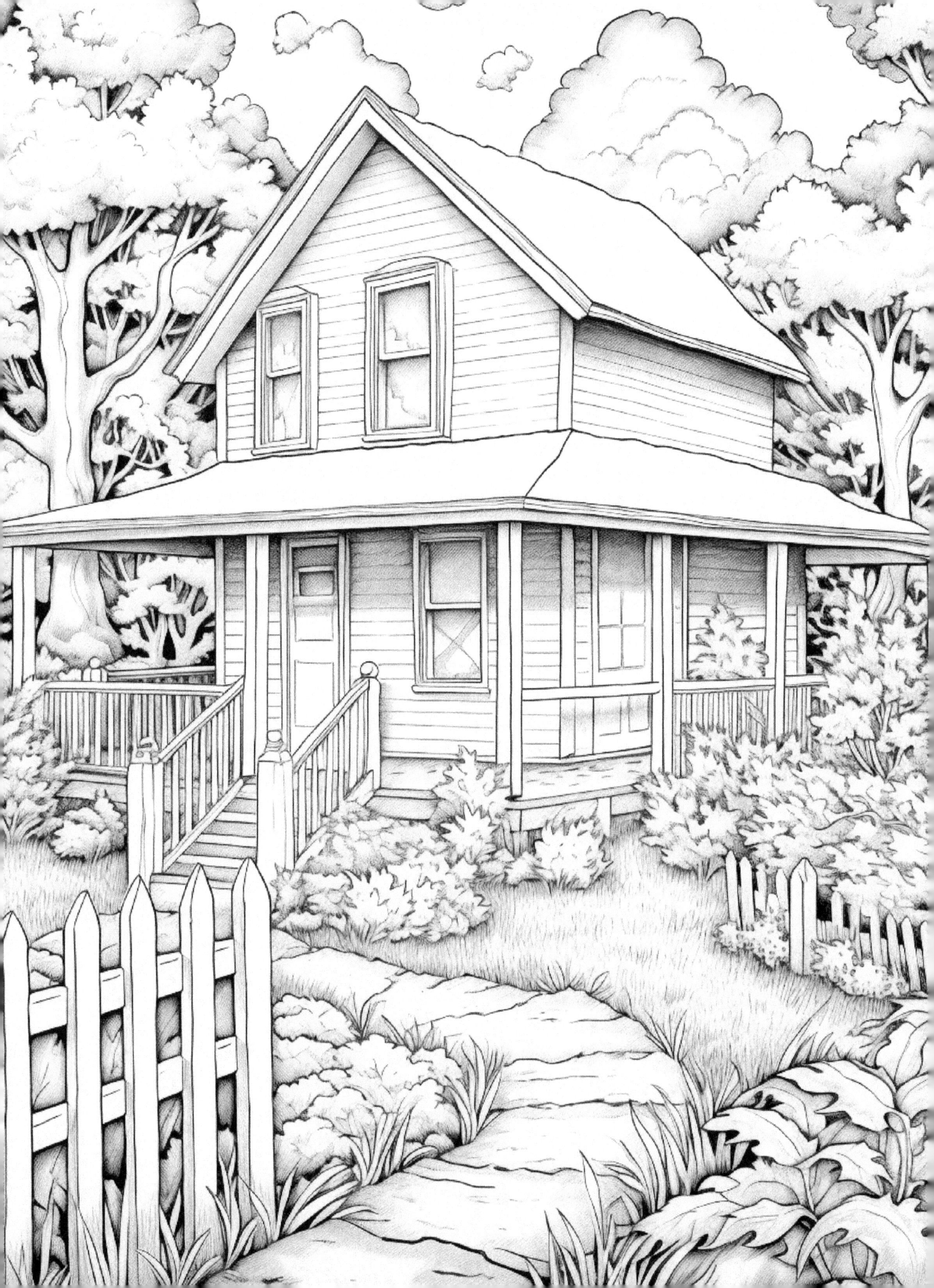

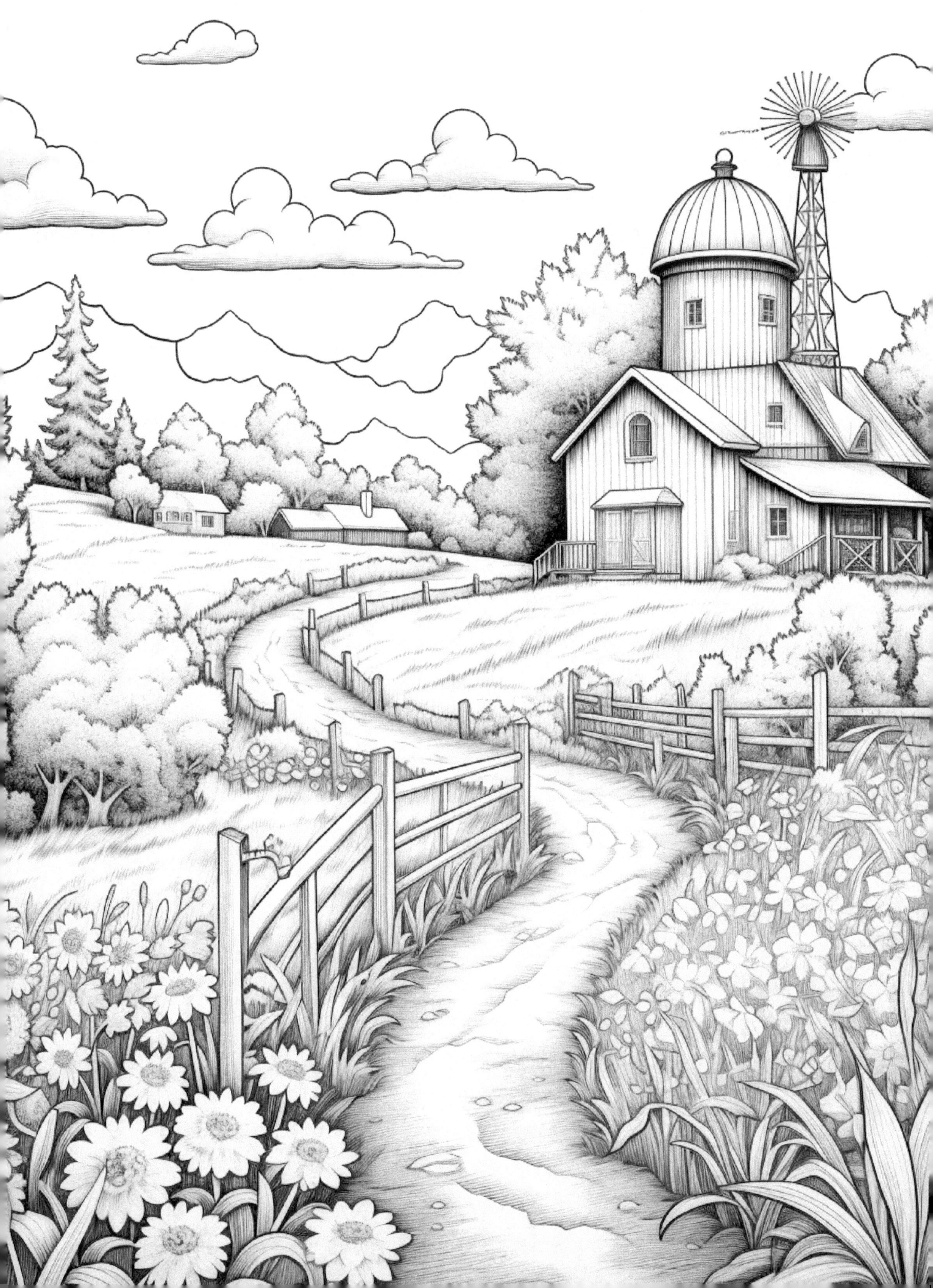

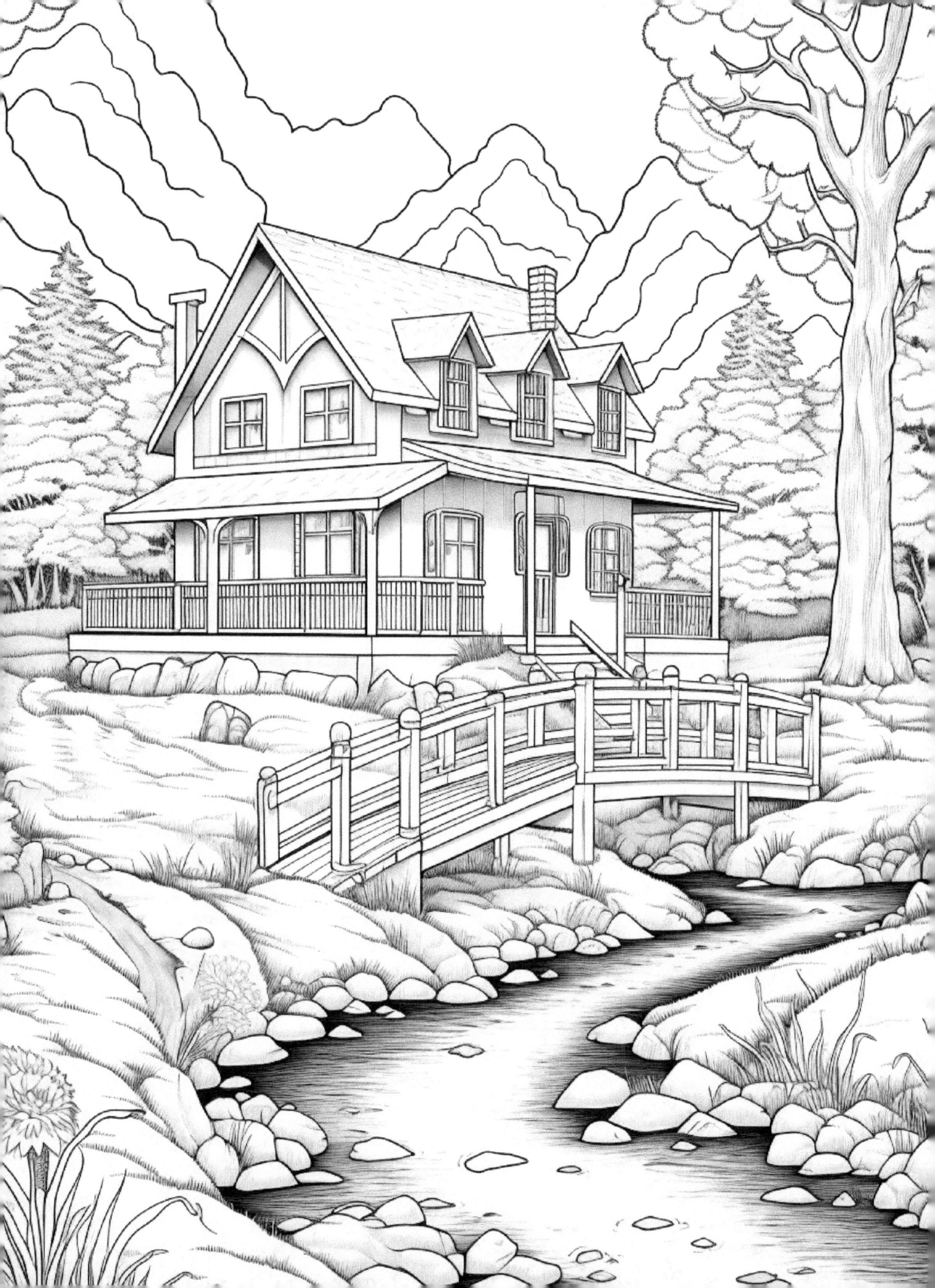

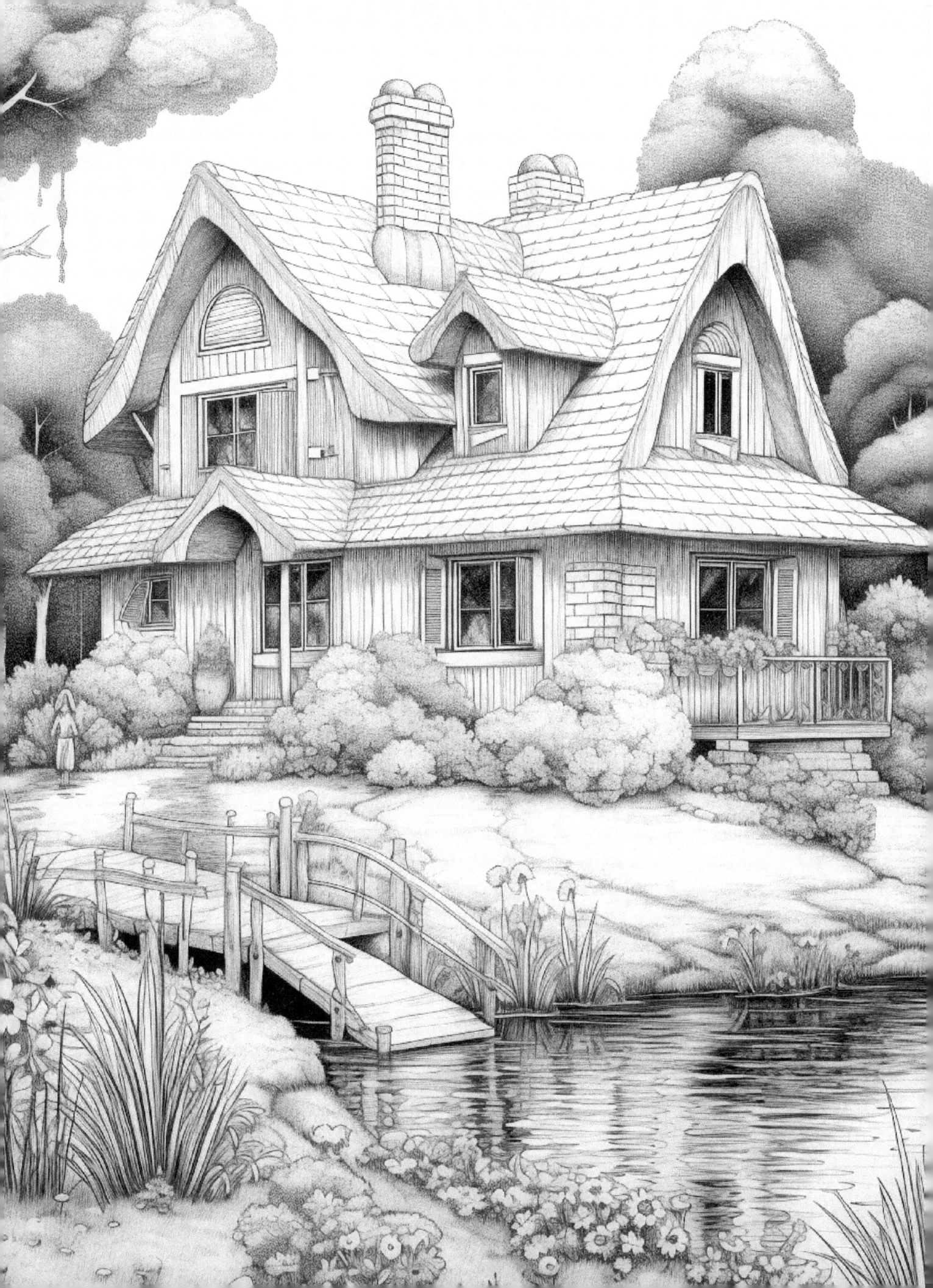

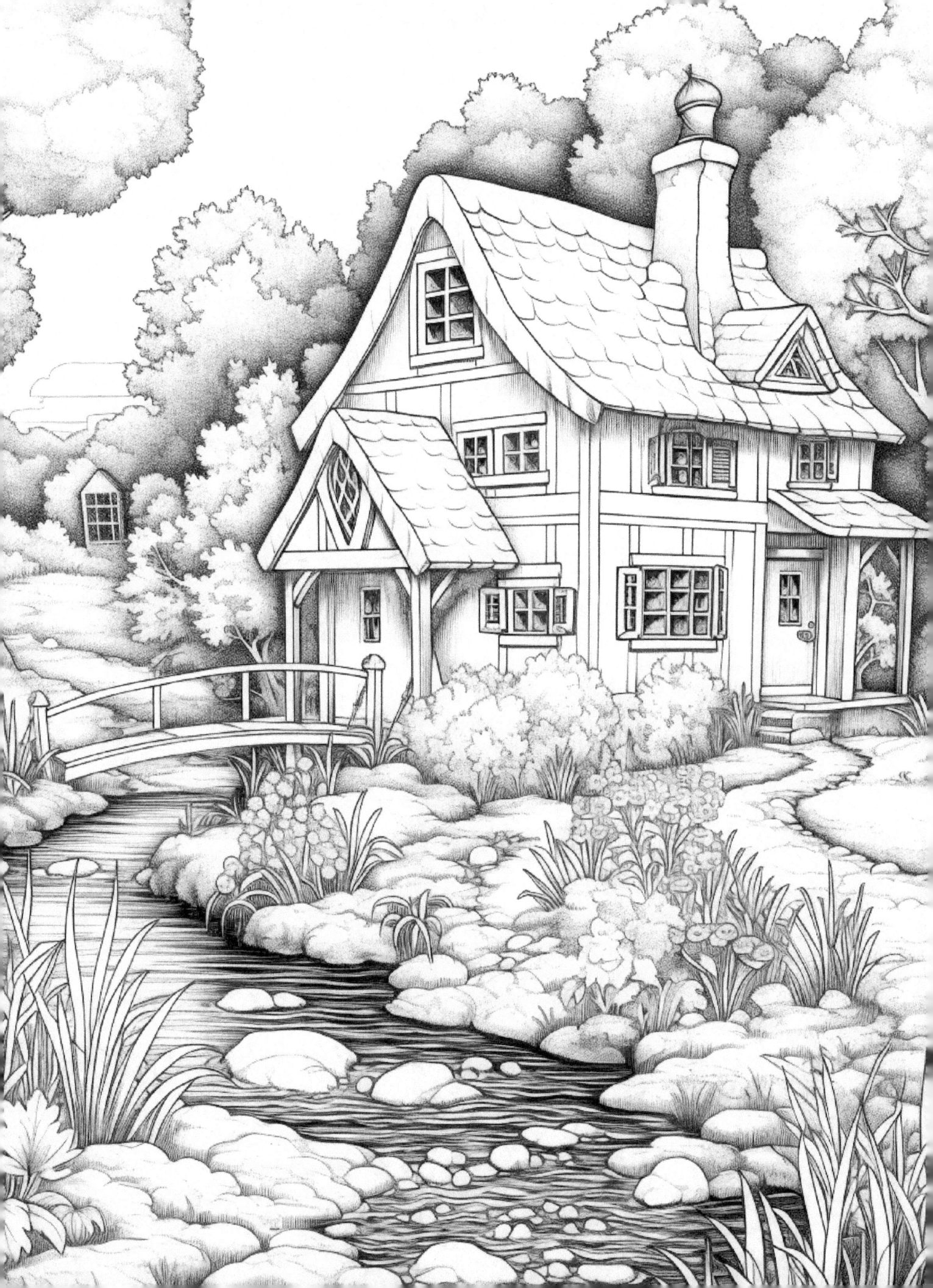

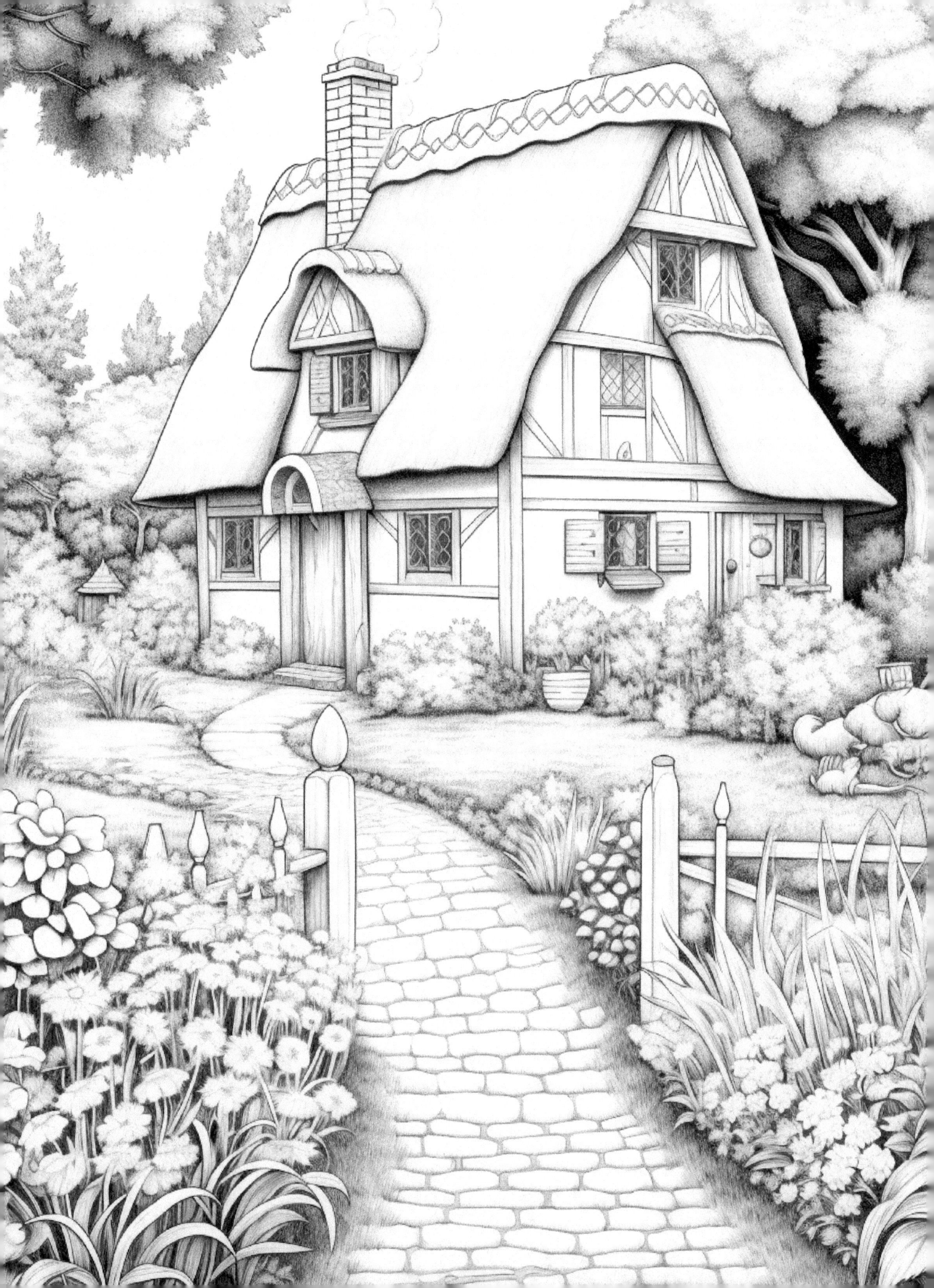

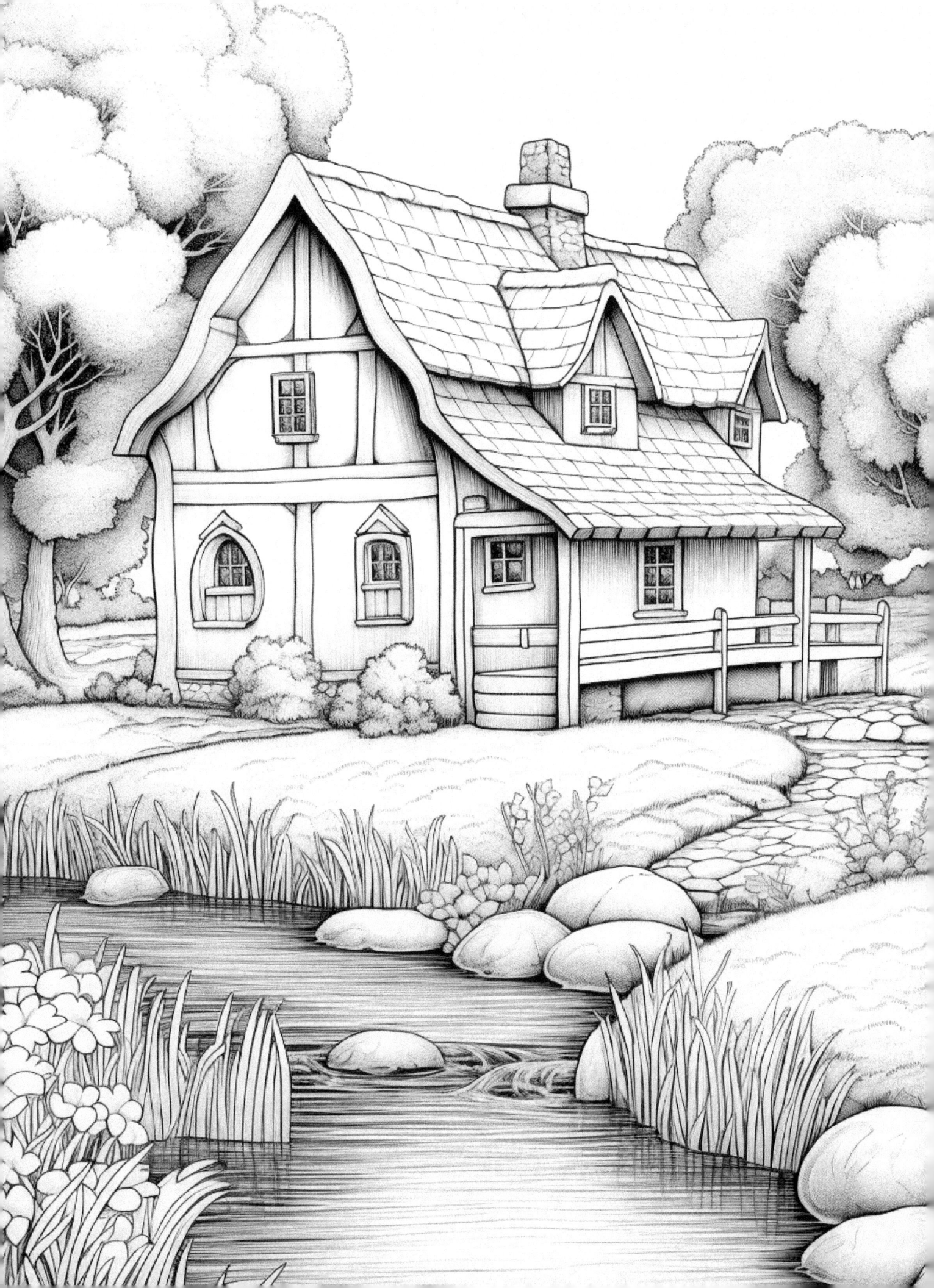

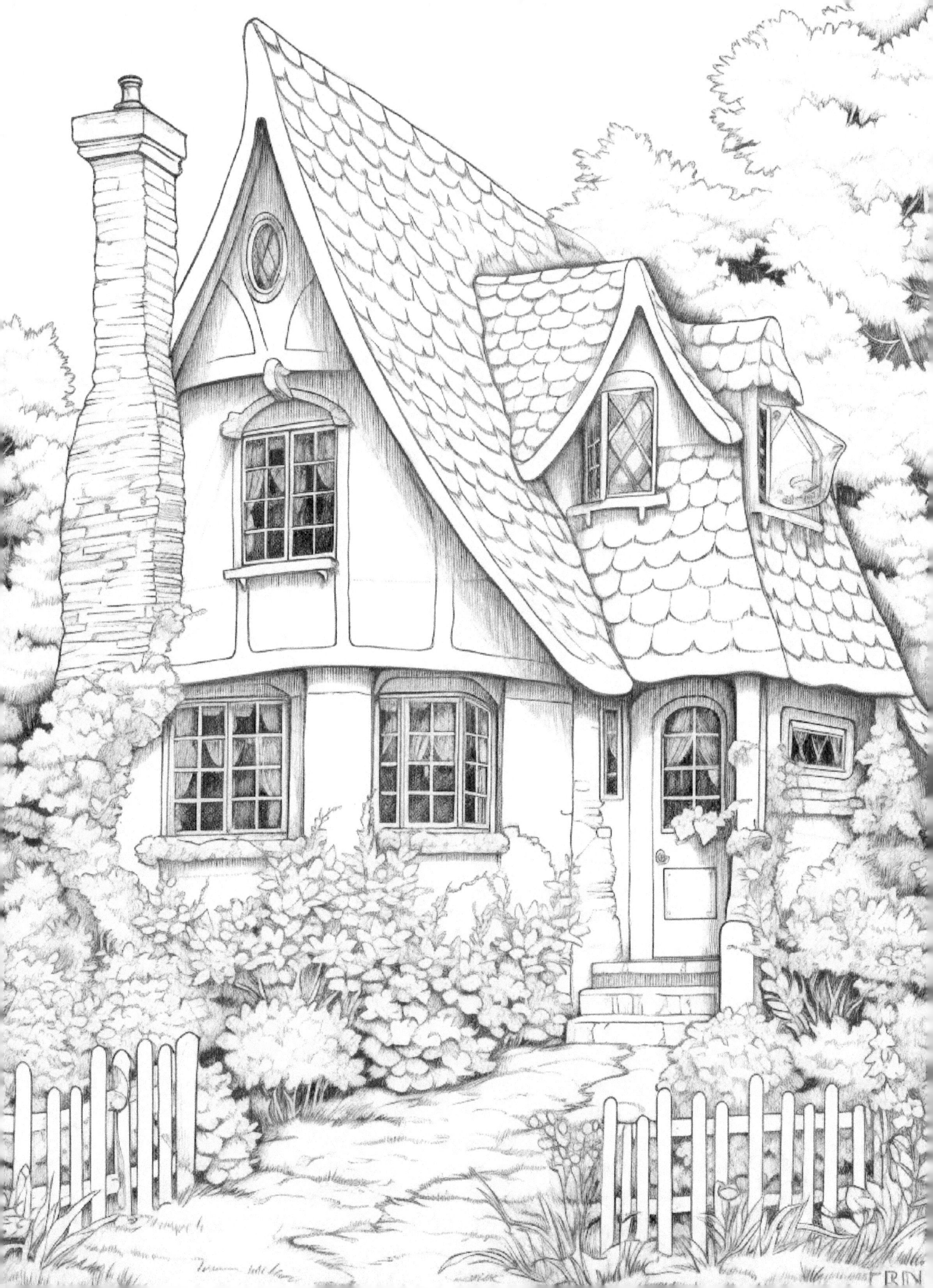

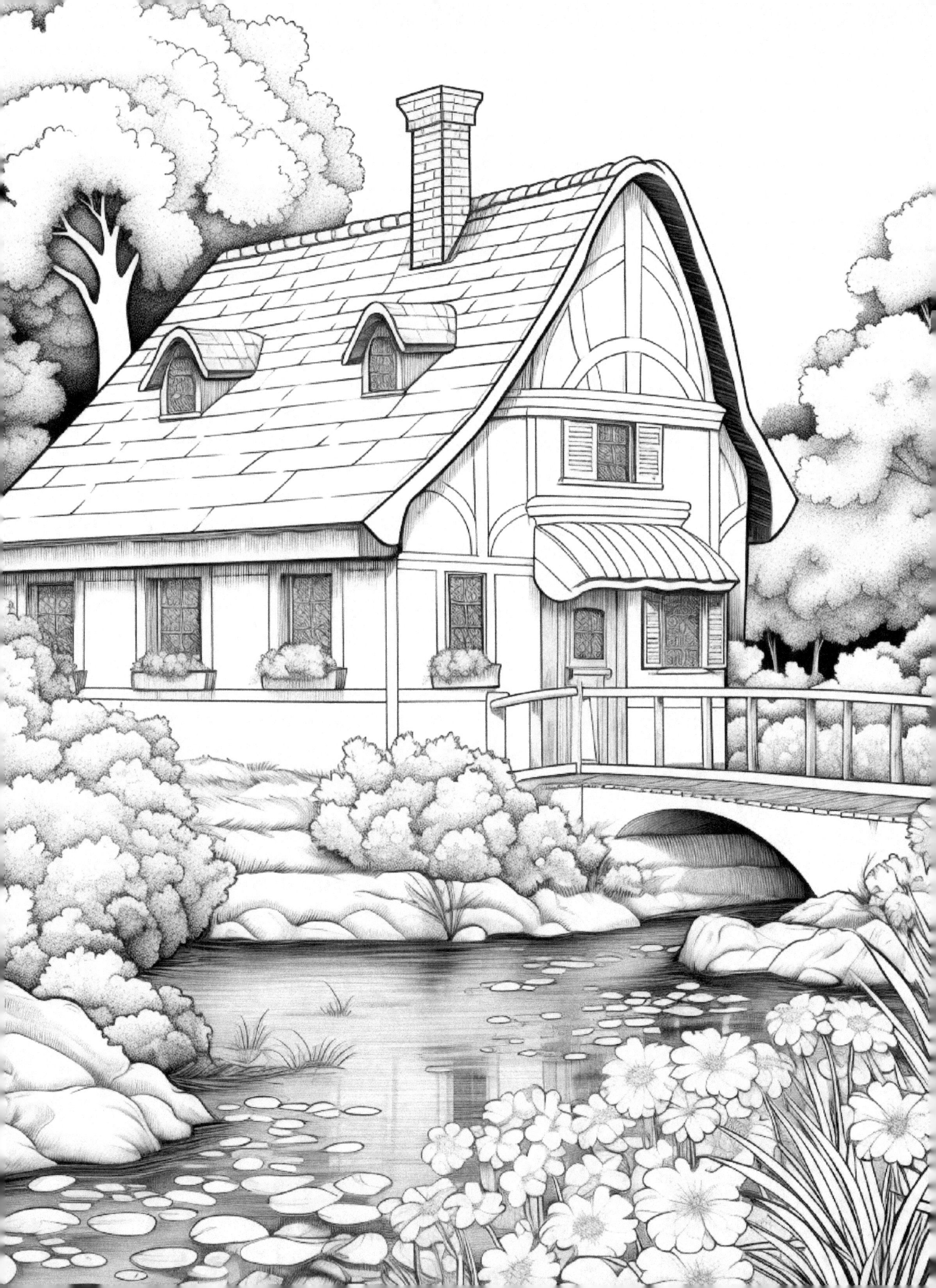

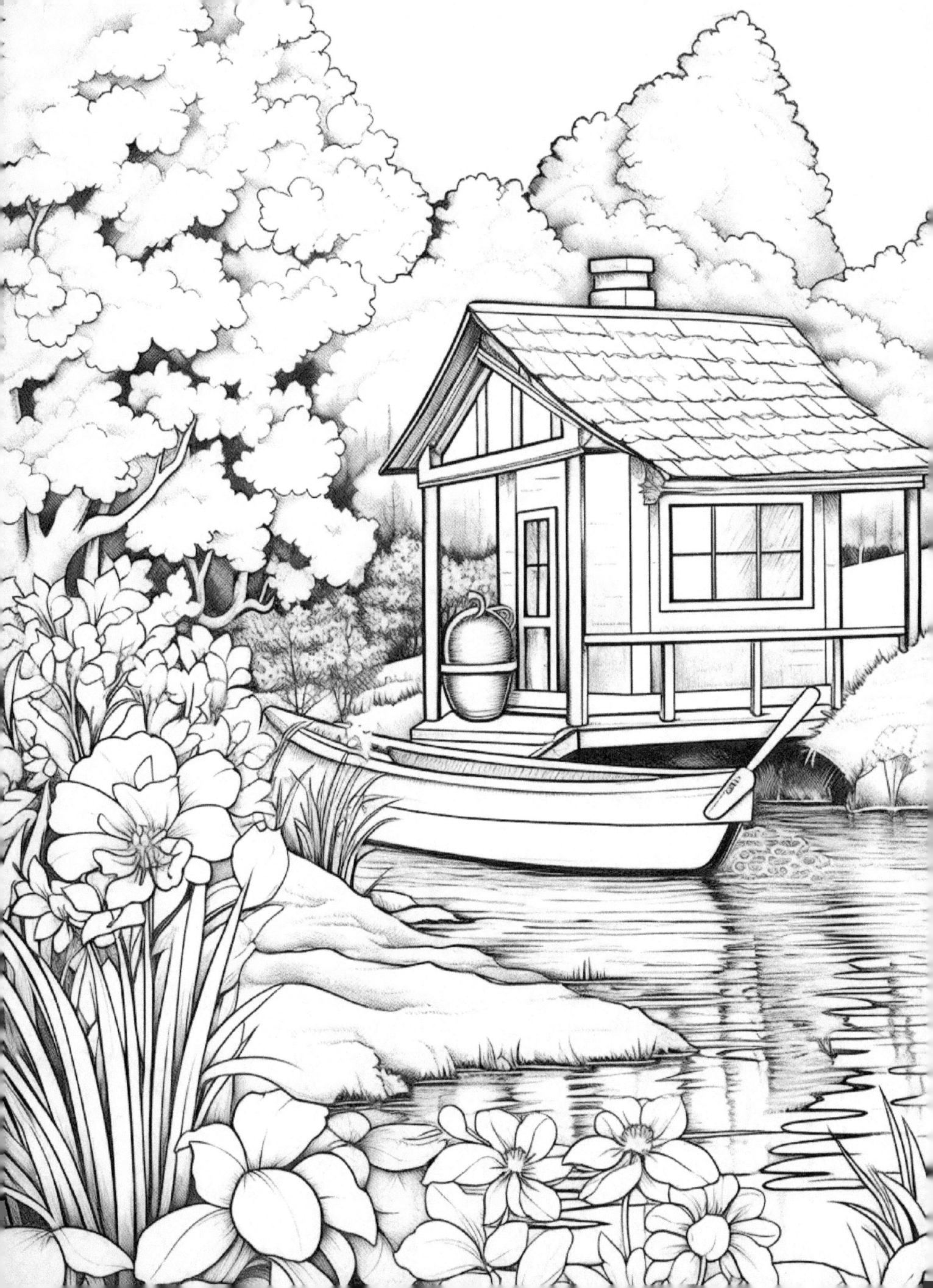

Thank You So Much For Spending Some Time Being Creative With Us.

Please take a look at some of our other activity, coloring books and journals

AH64Designs

www.ingramcontent.com/pod-product-compliance
Lightning Source LLC
Chambersburg PA
CBHW062127220526
45471CB00010B/3912